THE
LIFE
OF
A
GOSPEL
RAPPER

BY
Ahmed K. Handfield

Copyright   © January 2024 by Ahmed K. Handfield

Printed in the United States of America

Cover design and formatting by Ahmed K. Handfield

Published by Ahmed K.Handfield

Fayetteville, GA 30214

Karimforchrist@yahoo.com

Printed by Kindle Direct Publishing

ISBN 979-8-89184-294-6

DEDICATIONS

This book is dedicated to Almighty GOD, my wife (Michelle) and two sons (Jadon and Kierian), all of our living relatives, the entire body of Christ, every incarcerated individual in world who can understand the words on the pages of this book, and all those I have ministered these raps and testimonies to since 2005. I also dedicate this book to all people of all walks of life who have no faith in GOD at all, who are contemplating suicide, who worship themselves, those who don't want salvation, those whose faith is shrinking as the world gets worse, those struggling with drug/alcohol addiction, and those who feel that crime is the only way to get ahead or survive. I pray that I can change your perspective. When all is said and done only you can make the right choices for your life. May you succeed by fulfilling the will of GOD for your lives.

Be blessed.

Ahmed K. Handfield

ACKNOWLEDGEMENTS

I must greatfully acknowledge GOD Almighty for providing for me on every level of my existence. I also greatfully acknowledge my family for their loving support. My wife has supported me every step of the way in all of my music/ministry endeavors and has served alongside me over the years. Michelle is awesome. My two older brothers Keith and Alton have been the best big brothers I could ever have.

They have always cheered me on and loved me unconditionally no matter what. My son Jadon is always cheering me on and prays for me and his mother every day. I also thank you Sophia Gethers for encouraging and assisting me to write this book and getting it completed. Reader, you wouldn't be reading this book had it not been for GOD speaking through her to me to write it.

I acknowledge my awesome GOD Parents James Sr. and Jeanie Trotter for being there for me in my parents' absences from my life. I also acknowledge my church family at Fayette Family Church in Fayetteville, GA.

I acknowledge my Pastor and First Lady Jerry and Susan Young, Praise and Worship Pastor and his wife Lenny and Sally Beresford, and Finette and Howard Beresford. All of these amazing people prayed for me and coached, mentored, and groomed me into becoming a praise and worship servant.

They all have never stopped believing in me and helping me develop GOD'S gift inside me. I can't forget the praise team members that serve side by side with me on my favorite day of the week as we sing to encourage the congregation to hold onto GOD'S never changing hand. Also, I pray that GOD'S blessings be upon the loving congregation at FFC.

Lastly, I acknowledge every person that put me down in life. It only made me stronger.

Thank you.

TABLE OF CONTENTS

Introduction

THE LIFE OF A GOSPEL RAPPER
Introduction

Hi. My name is Ahmed K. Handfield (a.k.a. Karim for good life). I wrote this book to give you a break from the many offensive, verbally abusive, destructive, sexually explicit, violent, disrespectful, and immoral rap lyrics being blasted to the human race all over world. There is no way that I could shut this sector of the music industry down due to freedom of speech. As much as I dislike it, I can't judge the artists who put it out to the public. Here is what I can do.

I am offering you a refreshing alternative to this category of music. Feel free to call it (HIP HOP POETRY) if you like. Now, I have been inspired by Poets Such as: Nikki Giovani, Gil Scott Herron, and Shel Silverstein. I've also been inspired by old school rap artist such as Public Enemy, KRS-1, Rakim, Dougie Fresh, and a slew of other pioneers. I am most inspired by Gospel Rap Pioneers/ DJ's and Producers such as (Too Biz, Mark J, Elle Roc, Cross Movement, T-Bone, Lecrae, Trip Lee, The Go Ye DJ's, DJ Divine, Music Producer Mike Thomas), and many others. In this book I will share Godly rap lyrics with you for the purpose of deliverance, encouragement , and inspiration. You will see topics that cover intense issues our society is full of such as: praising GOD, suicide, whether or not to receive Jesus as Lord and Savior, faith, drug addiction, and encouragement for people (especially our young people) to stay out of jail.

You will see my personal true life stories and scriptural references with each rap.

So sit back, relax and enjoy a refreshing eyeful of lyrics that will either give you peace of mind, or challenge you down to your core to change for the better. I pray my true life stories behind these raps inspire you to keep loving and serving GOD or to start a new relationship with him for the first time. I have no judgement for you, for I am also to be judged by THE ONE who made us all. What I have for you is only love….. and love only. Oh, don't forget. As you read these raps do not expect perfect punctuation. I didn't write them with intentions to put them in a school English book for testing puposes. I just want you to get the flow. I typed the lyrics exactly how I minister them on the microphone in front of an audience. Yah know?

CHAPTER 1

GOD IS!!!

This first rap (GOD IS) came about after I decided to obey GOD. He told me to brag about him. I've walked in humility for many years after early years of pride and arrogance. I realized later in life that I am nothing without the love, grace, mercy, wisdom, and the divine heavenly protection of Almighty GOD. I am grateful for the blood of my Savior JESUS, and the daily companionship of the HOLY SPIRIT. I was also motivated to write this particular rap after hearing so many rappers, (including my old self), talk about ourselves. The reality is GOD is the one who puts breath in our lungs 24/7- 365 days a year.

HE gave us all tongues, teeth, and lips to speak. HE gave us a brain to formulate all the words that would come out of our mouths. Don't forget the most important part though. He can shut anyone of us down in less than a the smallest measure of time. Uuuuhhhhhh...... I believe it would be wise to praise GOD instead of our limited and temporary fleshly existence. Just think about it for a minute. All of us will die one day. Then we will begin to smell really bad shortly after we take our last breath on earth. Ha Ha!!! You think breaking wind is bad. You ain't smelled nothing yet. We think we're all that and a bag of chips. In the future we become the contents of a body bag that not even the Sanitation Department wants to touch.

Anyway, GOD is eternal and immortal. Since HE has that title HE deserves all the praise. We are nothing without him. During prison ministry and working in the county jail simultaneously on two different platforms, I came across a prayer book that is circulated throughout the prisons, county jails, and youth detention centers all over the U.S. One of the prayers focused specifically on the many attributes of GOD.

That alone gives us multiple reasons to praise him. I enjoyed that praise prayer so much that I turned it into a full length rap. YEP! GOD is that good. I know that JESUS will return any second now if I ever won a grammy after recording this particular rap. The reason I say that is because of the blatant fact that the world encourages everyone to worship ourselves in our own glory or (MY TRUTH). The majority run with it too. Well, my response to that type of behavior is…….Nah, I'm good WITH JESUS!!

GOD IS

Verse 1

My GOD is Adonai /Jehovah. He's my advocate....All in all!
Seeing me without he aint having it. GOD is my
anchor...his presence angelic...High Priest....Apostle... All
HIS greatness I can't tell it. If I gathered all the oceans,
streams, rivers, and lakes… turned them into ink,
however much it would take…. then tried to write of all the
greatness of GOD'S glory…… I'm out of ink before I could
finish my GOD'S story. GOD is my armour..... author of
our faith....the balm of Gilead. He's the banner for the
nations.....blessed.... the bright morning star. HE'S the
Captain..... salvation giver..... the ultimate chaplain......the
champion….. host......the LORD...... chief cornerstone
chief shepherd CHRIST.....the power.... The One all alone,
GOD is consuming fire... the cover from The
Tempest.....deliverer…… greater than the book of
Guinness World Records. His record is Universal/
Galactic..... greater than any human, plan, scheme, trick or
tactic. GOD is Emmanuel… GOD with us…. faith and
truth.... father of mercy……He's given us

(HOOK)- GOD is whatever I need. I'm ah give him
praise… Acknowledging him in all of my ways.

Verse 2

GOD is the ultimate flame that burns in my heart….at the same time, the fountain of living water. He's a work of art…A friend who sticks closer than any brother…. closer even than mother. I compare him to no other. GOD is glorious… all comfort… all grace… Lord of Host… Lord of peace….. Author of our faith. GOD is my light/my true Judge of All. He's the governor/High Priest. My soul, HE'S the lover of….. Great King over all the Earth. He's the king, above all GODS…. rules against all odds. GOD is the great light….The great shepherd of…. head of every man…. head over all things. He's the great I am. GOD is my help. He has all dominion…. Protector from the wicked…no respect for your opinion. High…Holy… Awesome…. all in one package. Spend time with GOD and life can't help but get impacted. Hope… glory…. provision… all part of the program…. making you feel better than the world's greatest slow jam. My sanctifier…my banner…my shepherd….and my healer….guardian, and my leader…..bonafide top speaker.

(HOOK) GOD is whatever I need. I'm ah give him praise…. acknowledging him in all of my ways.

Verse 3

My GOD is the LORD of host… LORD of peace… always there. He's above… never Beneath. He's the judge of the living and the dead…..the lamb in the midst of the throne….. always in my heart and my head. He never leaves me alone. The spirit that gives life…. the light of the world. He brings your life in order when your world swirls out of control. LORD (OUR MAKER). He made you then HE broke the mold. He holds you up when life starts to fold….. Omnipotent all powerful, mighty in battle. (JESUS CHRIST OF NAZARETH) is his handle… the Maker….the Mighty…..Redeemer….Love….the Mediator….(BETTER COVENANT) HE'S the author of…. the Messiah….Most Holy and Most High. Coming back to take us to Heaven breaking through the sky. GOD is my Rock…my Refuge…..my Salvation…my Shield Ya'll. JESUS is real ya'll. GOD is the Way, the Truth, the Testator,Divine,The Wonderful. The Alpha, and the Omega. GOD is my Maker….. the Keeper…….. The Gentle. No way that I could finish. This is to be continued…..

 Biblical Scriptural reference for (GOD IS): *Exodus chapter 3:verses13-14 & Jude chapter 1: verses 24-25(KJV)*

CHAPTER 2

KEEP YOUR FAITH

The only way I make it through life is living by faith. Without faith it is impossible to please GOD. If I put my faith in my job, my money, my talents, or my connections with other people I will fail in every area of my life. I refuse to ever again put my faith in these substitutes. These are the reasons my faith is in GOD.

People are finicky, fickle, unforgiving, and quick to cancel anybody who don't think the same way they think…as if we should all be twins with attatched heads (OR ELSE!!!!!). I can't put my faith in the stock market. You could lose years worth of money investments in 24 hours or less. As an African-American man living in America I'd better have faith in GOD for divine protection. My life means nothing to some groups of hateful, demon-possessed people.

So by faith I trust and believe in GOD'S word found in Psalm chapter 91, Psalm chapter 23, and Deuteronomy chapter 28: verses 1-14. Man will let you down 95% of the time. GOD will never let you down.

KEEP YOUR FAITH

Verse 1

Worry, fear doubt, disbelief is the welcome mat for Satan, he's the infamous thief. He's the author of lack and insufficiency. To abundant life now he's the enemy. Numerous bills… numerous debts… numerous bounced checks… numerous telephone threats…...too many ulcers…migraine headaches… too much fear… too much drama for too many years… too much unbelief….. too many confessions of not being worthy...too much doubt...too much worry……too much lack of understanding of the fact that GOD's the Master of our financial planning…too much worry about our children. Are they gonna come home alive or is somebody gonna kill them. Too much worry about jobs…Will I get robbed? Is somebody gonna carjack my car? Now hold up ya'll, because GOD's still on the throne. He'll never leave us or forsake us. We're never left alone. Dropping the ball is not allowed. GOD gives all grace. Yo! You'd better keep your faith.

(HOOK) No more worry. No more fears. Who has kept you all these years? Get on your knees and face and keep your faith.

Verse 2

We can't forget who God is. We can't forget that within us the spirit of GOD lives. We can't faint in hard times and days of adversities. Without faith...GOD, we can't please. You mean to tell me you've got doubts about the same GOD that brought the children of Israel out with silver and Gold.... the same GOD who invented hot, warm, and cold......the same GOD of the hundredfold...... BEHOLD!!!! THE Ultimate Provider. HE'S the KING of deliverance... the GOD who gives all forgiveness. HE'S the GOD of the beginning and the ending... the GOD who can help all men to stop sinning. Worry and fear means you really don't believe like the rich young man who walked away sad and grieved. Just receive that when you ask it shall be given. GOD knows everything we need while we're living. So be of good cheer. GOD overcame the world. What is a bill when GOD made diamonds and pearls? Yo! What is a thief? Tell me. What is a murderer? Remember! No weapon is going to prosper. So Keep your faith.

(HOOK)

 No more worry. No more fears. Who has kept you all these years? Get on your knees and face and keep your faith.

Verse 3

There's no need to fear... no need to doubt.... no need to cry. This is a job for GOD El SHADAI. GOD is THE ONE with the cure for cancer. Whenever you're confused, GOD has all answers. GOD is the universal GREAT PHYSICIAN. GOD promotes us from low to high positions. GOD is the rock... our strength...the almighty. Never take Prayer and time in the word lightly. You want to see God move, give him your best offering. God never fails to deliver what he's promising. God keeps it real. He's number one. Why wouldn't he give you what you ask? He gave you his son, Jesus. It's not GOD'S character to abandon. After you've done all that you can just keep standing, and witness the fitness, strength in GOD'S power. Give and witness as he rebukes the devourer. Let go! Let God don't make life hard. God's plan for man on Earth is to live large. Never forget that God is in charge. Worry is a waste. Yo! never let go of your Faith. You're your faith

Biblical Scriptural references for (KEEP YOUR FAITH
Hebrews chap. 11: verses 5-6, _Psalm chap. 91 Psalm_
chap. 23

Deuteronomy chap. 28: verses 1-14

(KJV)

CHAPTER 3

SALVATION

When I first received JESUS I was already considered a positive rapper. However, I had to renew my mind with biblical principles so I would have something to write about as a new gospel rapper. I got a bible concordance. For those who have never heard of this kind of book I'll tell you about it. This book has every word in the bible in alphabetical order. It gives you all the book locations, chapters, and verses these words appear in.

Well, I started writing down this information for (Salvation) and several words relating to getting saved. Then something interesting happened. During this time I had a warfare dream one night. In this dream there were two stairways surrounded by darkness. I was on an elevator. When I arrived at the top level the elevator opened. I saw two different armies. One army consisted of Battle-Trained angels with indestructible armour all over their bodies.

The other army consisted of dirty nasty demons. Both armies were about 100 feet across from each other while staring intensely at each other. They were all positioned for war.

Of course I quickly walked to the side the angels were on. They immediately parted a space for me to enter their ranks. As I entered one of them took it's arm, put it across my chest, and gently pushed me behind it to give me total protection. They then started charging toward each other. Just as their swords clashed with sparks and a loud impact I woke up.

As tears rolled down my eyes I thanked GOD for my salvation. I thanked him for HIS serious, totally committed, undying love, and promise of divine protection. This became ours as a result of the birth, death, and undisputed victorious resurrection of my LORD and SAVIOR JESUS.

I did my best to give a picture of what that would look like to today's human society. Hey let me make you aware of how powerful and persuasive GOD ALMIGHTY is.

I am a former Orthodox Muslim with origins of beliefs from birth at the Nation Of Islam Headquarters in Chicago, Illinois on Stoney Island Avenue. My mother, may she rest in peace, and my living Father were both members of the 1st Nation of Islam in the U.S. in the early 1960's. Both my parents were originally church kids thanks to my great grandmother and my grandmother. Later they chose to flip the script and the rest is history.

My mom left my dad and moved to Chicago with me and my four older brothers. We were well acquainted with Elijah Muhammad, Muhammad Ali, Louise Farrakan, and our God Father Dr. Abdul Salaam.

I pray this rap leads you to eternal life. I've ministered all the raps in this book and my other raps and songs countless times in churches, community events, prisons, county jails, youth detention centers, and most recently on Tik tok and Instagram under the name (Karim for Goodlife).

I pray you enjoy it. If you haven't decided to receive JESUS as Lord and Savior I pray you will before you leave this earth.

Salvation

Verse 1

There was a young brother who was running his games. He had wealth and fame. He made outrageous claims on the microphone about being a pimp/player/gangster. Spiritually he was a wimp. He came home 12 midnight… drank a 40 oz of alcohol. When it came to sin he did it all. He fell upon the bed. Into a deep sleep he entered. He heard a demonic voice screaming, "Grab the sinners." He saw people running for their lives from the attacks. Then he saw satan with knives, chains, and gats with a gang of demons. Then God's angels appeared. He was losing his mind. He screamed. He trembled. He feared. He saw God's angels in combat formation. One said, "Protect only the ones with salvation." He said, "Wait! I want that! Give it to me." The angel said, "Open your mouth and after me repeat."

(HOOK)

Don't you know that salvation is something you should never waste. Put your sin down, come to Jesus, and get in your rightful place.

Verse 2

The angel said, "It's not time for you in heaven yet. We've got a list of souls for you to go and get." He came back to Earth. The Holy Spirit moved in and tightened up all shortcomings and loose ends. He asked the Holy Spirit, " Who paid for my salvation?" The Holy Spirit said, "Jesus, the foundation." They jumped in an SUV and started cruising. The Holy Spirit counseled him for spiritual improvement. They passed by Temptation Avenue and Sickness Boulevard. Sin Parkway was extremely large. The Holy Spirit said, "Sin is very expensive." "So, remember the God in you cannot be tempted." The brother said, "How come I didn't die in my wicked ways?" The Holy Spirit said, "God wants all to be saved." "But we choose righteousness or wickedness…. bondage or freedom." " We choose to love God or to leave him."

(HOOK)

Don't you know that salvation is something you should never waste. Put your sin down, come to JESUS, and get in your rightful place.

Verse 3

As they cruised down the narrow Salvation Avenue they passed by wisdom, faith, strength, and truth. They saw countless testimonies of forgiveness. They saw great miracles and stores for God's business. God gave his only begotten Son. Whoever believes in him shall not perish. No. Not one. And if you sin repent Because you're redeemed….justified freely, then God's grace is on a scene to intervene. Jesus is the way. We can't deny this. Coming by any other way….Don't even try this. You're wasting your time. Send a post call to all. Salvation is a toll free call to Jesus for those who ball and pimp….like to get your freak on…those in bondage and sin….spending your every week on. The brother woke up, went to church, and got saved. He escaped satan's fiery grave.

Biblical reference scriptures for (SALVATION) Romans Chap.10:Verses 9-10

(KJV)

CHAPTER 4

SUICIDE

As a 16 year old teen my life was not what I thought it would be. During my teenage years my mom struggled with drug and alcohol addiction. Prior to her addiction she taught me how to survive without getting into trouble or doing something stupid to mess my life up. I'm so glad she did.

She also gave me and my brothers a good life before her addiction. I just wish she had done that for herself. Later when she passed away she was sober and clean, and she had given her life back to GOD. She held onto JESUS until her last breath. I know she's resting in peace now. During my teens we moved frequently. I always needed food and clothing.

Low income accommodations were the norm. I had no contact with my Dad at the time. My eldest brother Alton stayed with us for a little while so he could help us as much as he could. He once had to fight off neighborhood morons and bullies. I still remember our 1st eldest brother Arnold who passed away during the pandemic. He protected us from morons and bullies in Chicago before we all moved to Florida. Arnold also saved my life twice when I was a baby.

I would be missing my mom for days at a time. My friend Talib from high school along with his family would provide food and shelter for me from time to time. I cried by myself in the high school cafeteria after all the other kids would be gone. I didn't bother people and I kept to myself. When guys tried to bully me at school I would beat them up instead. I tried to end my misery on two different occasions. Once I swallowed an entire pack of sleeping pills one by one.

I only got a short nap out of that effort. The second/last attempt was by me swallowing a poisonous liquid. I only had a nasty taste in my mouth.
I finally realized and accepted that GOD wants me to live and use my talents/gifts to thrive in life and give hope to others. Decades later he has helped me to do just that by HIS grace and mercy. The bottom line of this rap is: DON'T GIVE UP!!

We have a lot to live for. Others can benefit from whatever gift that was downloaded into our existence by GOD Almighty Himself. Live your life for HIM. You are important whether you fell like it or not. I pray GOD'S best for you.

SUICIDE

VERSE 1

Hey! I can breathe. I can feel. I can see. I can taste. I can touch. Yo! That's what's up! Hey! Everyday that's above ground is a great day. 1st Priority is: I've got to pray. So, I say, "Lord thank you for the breath that I breathe." "Thank you." "Thank you for helping me to believe you, Jesus." "Thanks for life….so much to achieve." "God it's your presence I just can't leave." See, I don't have time for crying every night over my life about all the things that didn't go right. Man it is what it is. What's done is done. The past is gone. Now it's time for me to move on. Now death starts in your mind, but there is a resurrection. Provision is already made for the God connection. Life and death is in the power of your tongue. So choose life. You'll live to be a 101. Hey… suicide is not an option. When I chose Jesus I chose life….the greatest adoption. I have much to look forward to. Tough times I made it through. Giving up is something I can't do.

(HOOK)

Suicide I don't want your rides. I've gotta keep living everyday of my life. Suicide I don't want your rides. Man, I got to keep living. I've got to keep giving.

Verse 2

It's easy to be depressed and stress instead of focusing on all the reasons that I'm blessed… sitting back thinking about myself. Oh no! I've got to think of ways that I could help somebody else. Our bodies belong to God. Our bodies are God's property. So we've got to use them properly. Suicide is physical vandalism. So choose life. instead of the fire eternal prison. I don't have time to do myself harm…. put a bullet in my head… Shoot a needle in my arm…. put a joint in my mouth…. or have unprotected sex… banging 28 juicy freaks out…. that's not what life is about. People playing sexual Russian roulette. You lay down with strangers and aint no telling what you will get… or driving under the influence of alcohol. Not only suicide on yourself, you killed them all. Hey, we have assignments on Earth to complete….a purpose for life. Our lives we must not delete. This insanity we can't afford. We shall not die. We shall live and declare the works of the Lord.

(HOOK)

Suicide I don't want your rides. I've gotta keep living everyday of my life. Suicide I don't want your rides. Man, I got to keep living. I've got to keep giving.

Verse 3

Most people don't recognize that they're blessed. So, I express my love for life with gratefulness. I have to praise God daily for what's going right. When I observe the less fortunate I see the light. Look at how your body functions. Is everything working. But you're still complaining. What if your health worsens? What if you had to wear a colostomy bag…. or one leg was working while the other one you had to drag… or what if you had to eat through a straw with the tube coming out of your chest going into the left side of your jaw? Come on! Knock it off! Man what's the matter with you? Get on your knees and give praises to GOD to whom praise is do. Hey, we pray for them and the love of GOD we display to them. Count my blessings and life ain't so grim. The devil comes to steal kill and destroy. To get you to kill yourself…that's his favorite ploy, but Jesus came that we might have life more abundantly. Hang on! Life changes wonderfully. Don't give up. Jesus Christ's tight. Believe you shall receive ya'll and enjoy life.

__Biblical Reference scriptures for (SUICIDE):__
__Psalm chap. 118: verses 17-18 (KJV)__

CHAPTER 5

FREEDOM IS GONE

One of the identifying purpuses for my existence is found here in this chapter. As a gospel rapper I quickly realized that this type of rap would not be the mainstream media #1 at all. I could care less though. I just want to fulfill GOD'S purpose for my life. I worked in a county jail for 8 years, 9 months, 3 weeks, 2 days, 12 hours, 10 minutes, 46 seconds, and 14 miliseconds.

Yes. I know the detailed service time as a correctional officer because it felt like I was doing time myself and (I AIN'T EVEN DID NOTHIN!!!!)- Translation: I have no police record at all as a jail resident. After leaving that job I needed psychological counseling. Many of my co-workers have passed away. I personally want to thank the Sergeant that fired me.

If you are reading this book please contact me on either Tik Tok or Instagram. I would like to send you a nice church style LOVE OFFERING. Hey Sarg! You know what? You're aaaallllllright!!!!! Ha Haaaah!! Ok, moving right along. If a jail resident cursed me out while simply doing my job I wouldn't curse them back.

However, they would soon find out that I'd placed a 2-3 week Block, Brace, and hold up on their desperately coveted Honey Buns (heart stopping pastries) and those Baby Mama Visits.

This was always a (cuss out the officer) consolation prize due to their irate actions the week before. Yes, not (cursing) but (cussin). Real ghetto-like.....you know what I'm sayin? Later they were puzzled when I would still supply their toiletry and other supply needs as long as it was in my job description without judgement or condemnation. Then they started asking me to pray with them before I would send them off to court. I would honor their requests before opening the hallway cellblock doors. I know I was risking my job. Many of them would come back with our combined prayers answered. To GOD be the glory.

Officers are not supposed to pray with the incarcerated. Oooops!!! Yo! I use to get about 10-15 well mannered and mild knuckle heads and take them to the multi-purpose room, do some gospel rap for them with an old school cd player, and allow them to give feedback about what they heard and how it made them feel. They would even start ministering to each other. We'd do that for 20 minutes. Then I would get them back to their cells, secure the doors, and go home at shift change.

My sergeant found out I was doing these things for a while. That was one of the reasons I'm no longer a C.O. It was there that prison ministry allowed me to live my dreams. Wesley (My Brother in CHRIST) from church invited me out to Jackson State Prison to rap and testify. It was well received. He then introduced me to Sam Conner who serves with Bill Glass Behind The Walls Prison Ministry. As of today I've been doing prison ministry ever since 2005

Larry Rowe, John Lance, Jim Harris, and Big James were my first prison ministry mentors. I started out with Bill Glass Behind The Walls, Fly Right Ministries with Jim Harris, Forgiven Ministries with Scotty and Jack Barnes, and a few others. We even flew on a private jet to some of these events with our late fellow servant and Military Veteran Pilot Walker Hester. May he rest in peace. GOD birthed (Freedom Is Gone) out of me. I even went to a recording studio with three of my fellow correctional officers C.Johnson, J.Miller, and J.Raymond. Mike Thomas produced the music for it.
I pray that this realistic depiction of some of what I witnessed discourages younger/older people from doing something stupid like….hmmmm…..I don't know…uuhhhh….GETTIN LOCKED UUUUUUUPP!!!!!! Life is already tough, but it's tougher when any of us do stupid stuff.

FREEDOM IS GONE

Verse 1

This goes to all the wanna-be-pimp-misters,gangsters, prostitute sisters, and all other listeners. I'm going to take you on a incarceration journey (THE JAIL LIFE). The numbers of young people in jail concerns me. 4 o'clock….on the lights pop in your cell block. Steel doors open. You line up to get a tray of slop. You might find somebody's hair in your food. People in line are rude, and you're privacy everyone intrudes. After you eat you return to your cell where you dwell with people under the devil's spell… (A LIVING HELL)! You're dealing with all kinds of crazy aggravation. Your situation is causing you to experience deprivation. Now you see the crime you committed wasn't worth being in jail. You swear you wish you had of gone to church. On the night you got locked up in the wrong place at the wrong time. You were doing the wrong thing. Now you were blind. Now your freedom left behind. Officers let you out of your cell to breathe from 7 to 9, or 9 to 11. You realize that your life was heaven. You wish you had of listened to the reverend.

HOOK-What do you do when your freedom is gone, ripped, and torn. Now you're saying, "Man, come on!!" You broke the law…did something stupid and wrong. Now you're on your knees saying, "LORD help me be strong!!"

Verse 2

As you sit in the cell you count the seconds… the minutes… the hours…the months…the years reflecting. Doors open. It's lunch time: (a sandwich…an orange… a cookie…some juice….365 days a year. Oh goodie!!! After lunch you're back behind steel doors. You find out your cellmate has AIDS… thinking it's dripping through his pours. Terrified by the thoughts you can't sleep knowing your cell measures only 8 by 7 feet. Man, you can't wait until the cell door opens again. Everybody comes out. Now you're back in the lion's den of thieves…rapists, murders…law breakers…chance takers animalistic violators. No friends you're in the world of doggy dog. Every man for himself. It's the jailhouse law. You eat dinner….come out again. This happens 7 days a week. 11 o'clock…lights out… you sleep! Every movement you make is closely watched. Literally timed by paper you're clocked. It never stops. Steel and thick glass doors constanly block. They're all controlled and operated by the jail cops.

(HOOK) What do you do when your freedom is gone, ripped, and torn. Now you're saying, "Man, come on!!" You broke the law….did something stupid and wrong. Now you're on your knees saying, "LORD, help me be strong."

Verse 3

The door opens. You come out thinking just another day having no clue of the madness that's headed your way. Somebody says, "Your dinner belongs to me!", grabs your food, sits down, then starts to eat. Your anger heats up like lava from a volcano. Now you're fighting over some generic mashed potatoes. The officers come in…spray you with mace directly in your face, then your wrists by handcuffs they brace. They're taking you to Lockdown while your face is burning. You can hardly breathe. Now you're really learning a painful, hard, tough, lesson. You've never been to THE HOLE. Over your head is a mark with 20 Million questions. You enter the cell. You hate this. You see an 8 ft 255 pound muscle bound rapist. The steel door slams and you start to puke. He looks you up and down and says, "Ooooo, you so cute!" You try to wake up. It's not a dream. It's reality. You're fed through a square hole with a latch opened with a key. 23 hours a day locked in your cell. You're only getting one hour out. WELCOME TO HELL!!!!

Walking with JESUS everyday can prevent us from becoming a jail resident. HE will even give us a warning in the form of a certain uneasy feeling in regards to who we hang out with and where and when not to go to particular places.

Biblical Scriptural references for FREEDOM IS GONE—Proverbs chapt. 12: verses 5-7 & Matthew chapt 25: verse 36 (KJV)

CHAPTER 6
PUT THE DRUGS DOWN

This part of my life has to be the darkest time. It all started when my Mom married a drug dealer in Riviera Beach, Florida. My step-dad was selling dope but he was very kind to me and my brothers. Later all my older brothers moved out except Alton. My other brother Keith had already moved out and was living with our Aunt Marie in West Palm Beach. He and my mom were not seeing eye to eye. He came to our house to say good bye to us. He decided to go into the Army.

My mother became enraged and tried to attack him with a baseball bat. Keith ran out of the door and took off down the street. In tears I darted out, jumped on my bike and caught up with Keith. I knew that it would be a long time before I would see my brother again. I saw him and hugged him because it hurt me to see him run away. He told me he would be fine and that he loved me very much. I got on the handle bars of my bike as he peddled us to the city bus stop. His bus finally came. As he got on the bus he looked at me and said, "I'll see you again little bro." I didn't see or talk to my brother for seven long years.

My mom decided to leave my step-dad and took me to Atlanta, GA. I didn't see Alton for 3 years. We moved in Atlanta so many times my brothers couldn't find us. We didn't have cell phones and internet access back then like it is now. Keith told me later in life that he came to Atlanta as often as he could and just call different schools trying to find me. He even walked around in downtown Atlanta hoping he would by chance see me walking by.

Man we sure could have used a cell phone location app back then. He would leave heart-broken time after time because our instability kept me going from school to school. In my last year of high school my Counselor Patricia Mcjunkens told me to contact the RED CROSS to find Keith. I finally reconnected with my big bro in 1989. We have been in touch ever since.

During the multiple moves and relocations throughout the Atlanta area, there would be long periods of time when I would not know where my mother was. This led to me being left to fend for myself with the people we were staying with.

At one time, one of the family members of the people we stayed with got drunk and tried to attack me. The other family member stopped him and talked sense to this man.They would say to me, "I don't know where your mother is, but we can't take care of you so you have got to go." "You're not our responsibility!!" They were right about not being responsible for me. Fortunately, Ms. Mcjunkins reached out to the Atlanta branch of The United Way Foundation and they found a place for me to stay.

I stayed with Miss Mattie Anderson, (one of the community senior citizens) until I graduated from high school by attending summer school. What made it even worse is I finally caught the chicken pox during summer school. Miss Anderson gave me as much Ginger Ale and Pink lotion that I could stand.. Nevertheless, I obtained my high school Diploma.

I immediately started working at grocery stores, construction sites and fast food restaurants. May GOD bless the Managers at the fast food places I worked in. They knew my situation and made sure I went home with food every time. The beautiful thing about my God, Parents Jim and Jeanie Trotter was they provided work for me through my godmother's Community-based organization called the Wholistic Stress Control Institute in Atlanta and my Godfather's Seabreeze, Car Care/ and Janitorial Cleaning Service.

During this time I helped my mom as much as I could as I was learning to take care of myself. When she went to jail. I visited and put money on the books. When she went to NA meetings or AA meetings, I went to support her. Later on in life she finally got cleaned up.

Then something awesome happened. My positive rap songs were selected in a nationwide contest to be on a cassette tape sponsored by a major soft drink company. I took the money from that and got my mom out of the dope man's house. I got us an apartment where she stayed clean and attended her meetings. She later got approved to move into her own place in the Senior Citizen High rise buildings.

For years after that Mama constantly cried and would repeatedly apologize and tell me how sorry she was about abandoning me with her addiction. She kept asking me to forgive her. I would always tell her that I loved her. I always would let her know I recognized that she gave to me more than she could ever take away from me. SHE GAVE ME LIFE.

I would then always tell her there is nothing that would ever stop me from loving her. She went on staying clean, attending college, and meeting and spending time with her grandchildren before she passed away. The last time I saw my mother alive was in hospice where I sang to her and read scriptures to her. I told her I loved her very much.

If you are the person struggling with drug or alcohol addiction ask for God's help. Please make a quality decision. Be there for your future and for your family. You could avoid a lot of hurt and pain in your life and theirs if you do so.

PUT THE DRUGS DOWN

Verse 1

No more pipes… no more needles….. no more joints. When it destroys your family, yo! What's the point? No more broken promises and let downs… no more leaving your family getting high out of town…. no more abuse under the influence…. no more hearts broken…. no more people's lives ruined…no more let downs or setups… No more abandonment… no more distrust… no more leaving your family bankrupt… .no more stealing. Enough is enough. Are you done? Are you done? Are you finished? Almost every relationship you had is diminished. Resources depleted. Defeated is your status. Over-dramatic! When will you put down that apparatus? What is your status? Take a long look in the mirror. The fact is that total destruction is nearer for you. Get off the train tracks cause the train is on the way. The time to change is today. Not tomorrow, not next week, but right now right now, right now. yeah, put the drugs down!

(HOOK)

Raise your families. Love your children. Stay in their lives. Put the drugs down!! Make a decision to be there for your loved ones. Don't make them cry put the drugs down!!

VERSE 2

I was a child… hopes dreams in my heart. It seemed that I was doomed right from the very start. Mom left dad and married a drug dealer. Little did I know she was a slave to the dealer's dope. When she couldn't cope with stress, it was a downward spiral of destructiveness. The dope man she later left. Our lives drastically changed. I cried when the left all of my friends. Life was rearranged. We lived so many places I lost count. Drugs took a toll at an alarming amount. I'd be awakened in the middle of the night… strangers in our apartment getting high like a kite. But I kept writing raps… kept dreaming. Mom's life seemed like it had no meaning. She was still feigning I got depressed… suicide…. 2 attempts! I woke up wondering yo! Where my mom went? Days turned into weeks… weeks to months. People put me out in the cold when all I wanted was a home. I hated that drugs came before me. She used to kiss me and hug me…tell me that she loved me.

(HOOK)
Heal this nation coast to coast. We can win!! Put the drugs down. We can make it. We will thrive. JESUS is on our side. Put the drugs down!!

Verse 3

Mr. & Mrs. Trotter forever I will love you. My God-Parents took me in… became my rescue. Once again I was able to laugh and smile. It's true it takes a village to raise a child. I tell people are over the Earth when you do drugs, your body is not the only thing that you hurt. You break hearts people depending on you to come through and do what you're supposed to do. Don't let yourself down. Don't let down those that love you. You can't do it on your own. Jesus above you will strengthen and you give you his power/resistance, super-natural help, healing, and assistance. You can make it. You can quit. Make a decision. Don't live a lifestyle of multiple collisions. Let it go!! You can't handle it on your own. Fathers, mothers, and loved ones come back home where you belong. That child is waiting for you with open arms. Don't make them experience hurt, shame, harm, neglect, pain,depression….no more LOST but FOUND. PUT THE DRUGS DOWN!! PUT THE DRUGS DOWN.

I pray this book blesses you and your loved ones for many generations to come. Peace and Love ya'll

ABOUT THE AUTHOR

Ahmed K. Handfield

Karim is gospel rap artist, beatboxer/vocal percussionist, singer, and song writer who is a born again Christian. He converted from the Muslim/Islamic faith by the love of Christ in 1996. He has been rapping and singing since 1984 from coast to coast in the U.S. and as far as Senegal, West Africa in churches, schools, youth detention centers, prisons, and various community events.

He was born in Rochester, New York, but he now resides in Fayetteville, GA with his wife and youngest son. He is a former Correctional Officer who worked 8 years in a local County Jail in his home state of Georgia He has worked in prison ministry since 2005 with the following ministries: Bill Glass Behind the Walls, Forgiven Ministries, Fly Right Prison Ministries, and Inmate Encounter Prison Ministry.

He currently serves with his wife on the Praise team of Fayette Family Church in Fayetteville, GA under Pastor Jerry and 1st Lady Susan Young.

The link below showcases one of Karim's raps in a video produced by V Labar Productions

(NOT ABOUT ME)

https://youtu.be/zNn3KtOFEgU

Email: karimforchrist@yahoo.com

Made in the USA
Columbia, SC
09 April 2024

34033535R00024